AF435349

My Bottle of Olive Oil

26 life-lessons squeezed from
the crushed olives in my life.

By

Dr. Thomas E. Chatman, Jr.

ISBN 979-8-218-05265-2
eISBN 979-8-218-05266-9
Library of Congress Catalog Card Number: 0000-0000

Published August 2022

Each of us is born with the potential to be the best version of ourselves, which includes reaching big goals and dreams. Unfortunately, potential alone does not guarantee these things will happen. Why? The answer is simple: LIFE. Life can present us with a variety of challenges that make it extremely difficult to move in the direction of our best selves. What's the big deal? It's twofold. Not living up to our true potential can affect our self-esteem and overall quality of life. In addition, when we do not live our lives to the fullest, we deprive the world of the associated benefits. For example, the airplane, cell phone, television, automobile, and many other modern-day conveniences can be linked to individuals who chose to live fully and pursue their dreams. Their decisions have benefited everyone and the same will be true for you if you choose a path that leads to the best version of yourself.

My Bottle of Olive Oil is a book about the wisdom and lessons I have gleaned over the last almost 50 years of my life. Negative experiences include being picked on in grade and middle schools; educational, professional, and financial setbacks; self-sabotaging behavior; anxiety; divorce; legal battles; emotional eating; sickness; and low self-esteem. On the positive side, I have found more peace and calm; earned a doctorate; lost weight; increased my self-esteem; and achieved personal and professional success. The book is titled *My Bottle of Olive Oil* because when olives are pressed or crushed, they produce olive oil. This oil can be used for many things including healing, cooking, and cleaning. The lessons or olive oil, if you will, reflect the good that came from every situation in my life. I believe the wisdom and lessons will benefit others who are undoubtedly striving to live their best lives and experience all that life has to offer. *My Bottle of Olive Oil* is packed with 26 short messages, starting with each letter of the alphabet, and it includes a section where I share a related personal experience. Each message ends with a challenge or a question that allows you to reflect on the message.

My Bottle of Olive Oil is also based, to a lesser degree, on my education and professional experiences over the last 30 years. My educational training beyond high school led to degrees earned in psychology, education, counseling, management, and family and marriage therapy. This knowledge provided tools for understanding human behavior and helping people reach their full potential in life. My professional experience includes being a public school teacher, minister, manager, executive advisor, professor, counselor, college administrator, life coach, motivational speaker, and business owner.

Although you may not find all 26 lessons relevant right now you should find a few that resonate with something you have experienced or are experiencing in life. My hope is that you will take time to reflect on the messages and the lessons offered and take steps to apply what you learn. As with anything, learning new behaviors can be challenging and scary. Give yourself time to fully embrace new ways of thinking and behaving. This will take patience and courage. There will be internal resistance, but it will subside if you persist. The final outcome will be a life that is filled with more peace and happiness as well as more personal and professional fulfilment.

To the best life you are intended to live,
Dr. Thomas E. Chatman, Jr.

DEDICATION

This book is dedicated to my parents, Thomas and Ruth Chatman. They have been by my side from day one and have supported me through every trial and triumph. They truly are the wind beneath my wings. I also dedicate this book to my three wonderful children, Brianna, Thomas III, and Brennan. I strive to live my best life because I am their role model. If I am not my best, I cannot be the best father. They are my biggest motivation. Lastly, I dedicate this book to the countless family members, friends, and colleagues who have encouraged and supported me through the years with their kind words and gestures. I remember and appreciate you.

<u>**Appreciate**</u> what you have right now because an abundance of peace, joy, and happiness awaits you.

Appreciating what you have right now, or as some say counting your blessings instead of your problems, is one of the most transformative things you can do in life. It is a shortcut to feeling better about a bad situation or life in general. This habit also leaves the door open for positive instead of negative things to happen. For example, when you realize just how fortunate and blessed you are, your level of expectation for the future changes. When this happens, you become a magnet for positive and good things happening. This positive and fruitful cycle continues as long as you always appreciate what you have.

My personal application:
I have a long, running list of all the things for which I am grateful and appreciative. I actually keep the list in a journal and a PowerPoint presentation so I can refer to it on a regular basis, especially during challenging and difficult times. Without fail, reviewing my grateful list lifts my spirits and makes things seem not so bad. It's almost like putting fuel in my mental and spiritual tanks when they are running low.

Your challenge/homework:
Make a list of 20 things for which you are grateful. To take this to the next level, create a grateful journal using a notebook or a composition book. By doing this, you can track, document, and reference the things for which you are grateful. Reviewing your grateful list is transformative and is definitely a game changer when nothing seems to be going right.

<u>Appreciate</u>

*Using the space below, make a list of 20 things
for which you are grateful.*

Believe in yourself because it
makes dreams come true.

B elieving in yourself is the single most important thing you can do to increase your chances of reaching your goals and making your dreams a reality. Your thoughts about yourself direct and guide your daily behavior and the actions you take in life. If you believe you can succeed at a particular task, you are more likely to try. If you believe you can overcome a difficult challenge, you are more likely to seek help to handle it versus being paralyzed by doubt and fear. Believing in yourself has the power to propel you into your destiny and help you achieve the unimaginable. It will make the impossible seem possible, the unthinkable seem thinkable, and the unimaginable seem imaginable. Finally, believing in yourself can serve as a buffer against criticism from others and second guessing by you. When you believe in yourself, you have the most important tool for success and winning. This singular act will push you to achieve much more than you or anyone else ever imagined.

My personal application:
I recently earned my doctorate after starting it over 30 years ago. The first time I attempted a doctorate, I did not finish it because of a host of life issues. As time passed, I started doubting whether I could ever finish it. After a major life event in 2016, I decided I had to set my mind for success in order to complete my doctorate. Finally, with a renewed belief in myself, prayer, and encouragement from others, I did it. When I wanted to give up or I became discouraged, my steadfast belief that I could finish my degree was one of the key factors that helped me cross the finish line.

Your challenge / homework:
Jot down one or two goals that you have not achieved because you don't really believe you can, and explore why you don't think you can reach them. Once you have explored the reasons, address each reason by stating the goal in the affirmative. For example, I can purchase a home or I have the capacity to manage my finances. Use these positive affirmations to help you build a strong belief in yourself.

Believe

Using the space below, jot down one or two goals that you have not achieved because you don't really believe you can, and explore why you don't think you can reach them. Once you have explored the reasons, address each reason by stating the goal in the affirmative.

<u>Celebrate</u> every success, great or small, because it leads to more success.

Celebrating success is similar to being grateful and appreciating what you have right now. Reaching big goals in life is no small feat, and the thought of doing so can be paralyzing at times. For example, when you look at the goal and all the things that have to be done to accomplish it, you can easily become defeated even before you start. One strategy for achieving big goals is to celebrate the small successes along the way. Celebrating and charting small successes toward your goals and dreams can be a source of motivation and encouragement to keep going until you finish. Celebrating success milestones builds confidence and momentum, which will help you finish what you started. The more you celebrate, the easier it becomes to reach your goal.

My personal application:
Getting to my goal weight has always been a challenge for me. As such, I keep a close eye on my goals and the small progress I make. If I lose a pound, I celebrate. If I work out, I celebrate. If I opt for a healthy meal over an unhealthy one, I celebrate. Celebrating these small successes keeps my momentum up and helps me to keep pushing, especially when it seems like it's taking forever to reach my goal.

Your challenge/homework:
What is one goal you have that you have yet to reach despite your best efforts? Break down the goal into as many parts as possible. Use all the parts as milestones that can be celebrated when they are reached. Reaching and celebrating the milestone should serve as fuel to help you finally reach the goal.

<u>Celebrate</u>

What is one goal that you have yet to reach despite your best efforts?
Break down the goal into as many parts as possible.

____

____

____

____

____

____

____

____

____

____

____

____

____

____

____

____

<u>Devote</u> yourself to the process of becoming successful because it guards against quitting.

Devote means to give all or a large part of one's time or resources. For example, you devote several hours each day to completing a special project. The act of devoting yourself to the process of becoming successful means you embrace the associated ebb and flow that comes with it. Instead of viewing issues as obstacles, you view them as opportunities and forge ahead. Why do you this? Because you appreciate that challenges and obstacles are par for the course, so to speak. True devotion to the process of becoming successful will help you press past the highs and lows on your journey and keep you from quitting when you experience a road block or a setback.

My personal application:
Completing my dissertation for my doctorate was an extremely big goal for me. I knew without total devotion to the process, I would not complete it. Prior to starting the writing process, I did some research to understand what people typically experience when they are completing a dissertation. Once I had a handle on the expected ups and downs, I braced myself and committed myself to the process. It was this stance that allowed me to push through to the end. The devotion to the process made the difference. Without it, I would not be Dr. Chatman today.

Your challenge/homework:
Identify one or two goals that you are having difficulty reaching. For the goal, research the process involved in reaching it. The research can involve personal interviews with people who have reached the goal or reading about people who have reached important goals. Use the information you gather to help keep things in perspective as you work toward reaching your goal.

<u>Devote</u>

Using the space below, identify one or two goals that you are having difficulty reaching. For the goal, research the process involved in reaching it.

<u>Expect</u> great things to happen in every situation because this directs your actions and thoughts.

Many studies have been conducted to demonstrate how a person's expectation in a given situation actually influences the outcome. For example, when people believed in a certain outcome, that outcome was more likely. Additionally, it was noted that their actions and behaviors were consistent with the expectation they had. Therefore, if someone expects to fail a test, there is a good chance they will. Conversely, if a person expects to succeed at a task, they usually will. So it is critical, no matter the situation or circumstance, that you expect a positive outcome. This mindset guides your actions toward the expected outcome and positions you to win every time.

Your challenge/homework:

My personal application:
When I was in graduate school at the University of Minnesota in the late 90s, I had to take and pass a comprehensive exam in order to earn my master's degree. I was talking to a classmate a few weeks prior to taking the exam, and he expressed doubts about passing the exam. Although I was nervous about taking the exam, I dug deep in my spirit and adopted a positive attitude and stated that I expected to pass the exam. Fortunately, I passed the exam, and unfortunately, my friend did not. Did our different expectations make the difference? Although I cannot prove it, I would like to believe that my positive expectation gave me a slight edge as I prepared and actually took the exam.

Your challenge/homework:
List two or three things that you have coming up in the next week, month, or year and create a positive expectation statement for each thing. Put it in a journal or post it somewhere you can review it each day. Make a note of how things turn out and note any differences you think having the positive expectations made.

<u>Expect</u>

Using the space below, list two or three things that you have coming up in the next week, month, or year and create a positive expectation statement for each thing.

<u>Focus</u> like an eagle when pursuing your goals
because it guards against distractions.

One of my favorite pastors once said men fail because of broken focus. This has never been truer. Many folks spend countless and unnecessary hours on a task or goal because of their inability to focus. Although focusing on a task or a goal may seem very simple, it is not. It takes courage and discipline. When we focus, we must tune out distractions from others and the environment. This can be very challenging if you are sensitive to distractions and background noise. If you are going to accomplish anything worthwhile, you absolutely must focus like an eagle. When you do, it ensures you get the task or goal completed in a timely manner. The company Amazon that employs individuals to deliver packages to customers pays more per hour to those who are able to focus and deliver packages quickly. An eagle has an extraordinary ability to focus on its target and seize it. With an eagle's focus, you too can seize upon your target and accomplish more in life.

My personal application:
I am embarrassed to say that I have been on the weight-loss rollercoaster for many years. I would lose some weight and then before long and without even realizing it, gain it back. After the last rollercoaster ride and gaining back all the weight I had lost and then some, I jumped off the rollercoaster and investigated why I was going up and down. The answer was a lack of focus. With journaling and staying consistently aware of my goals, I am able to maintain my focus now. I have finally reached a weight-loss milestone and have been able to maintain it longer than I have in the past. My increased focus has made the difference.

Your challenge / homework:
Note a goal or task that you have yet to complete and you suspect a lack of focus to be the culprit. Ask yourself what distractions are keeping you from completing it. Next, develop a strategy for how you can incorporate a system for maintaining the necessary focus to complete the task (journaling, using a timer, calendar, graph, accountability partner, etc.).

Focus

Using the space below, write down a goal or task that you have yet to complete where you suspect a lack of focus to be the culprit. Ask yourself what distractions are keeping you from completing it.

<u>Give</u> back and help others often because it heals you and others.

On the surface, giving back or helping others may seem like it's just helping the recipient. This does indeed help the recipients and allows them to benefit from resources they would not have otherwise had. In other words, giving helps sustain us in a world where access to resources is not always available. The other part of giving back or helping others that is equally important and powerful is the benefit to the person who gives or helps. Helping others has a way of lifting your spirits and helping you appreciate just how fortunate and blessed you are. Many people who help others experience a positive shift in how they view the challenges in their lives. Sometimes helping someone is all that a person needs to do in order to get out of a stupor or to end a pity party. So give back often. It will help you, others, and the world at the same time.

My personal application:
On occasion, life hits me pretty hard or I just have a season when I am not feeling particularly great about how things are going. The one thing I have learned over the years is that helping someone always makes me feel better about my life or current situation. Since life gets busy and helping others on a consistent basis can fall by the wayside, I build time and/or activities into my schedule that involve helping others. By planning this, I ensure that I have a buffer in place to help me keep things in perspective and to move forward. I cannot overemphasize the importance of helping others. It's indeed a win-win situation.

Your challenge/homework:
Identify one thing you can do, that's not required, that would reflect giving back or just helping someone. Once you have identified it, build it into your schedule and watch the benefits start to add up.

Give

Using the space below, identify one thing you can do,
that's not required, that would reflect giving back or just helping someone.
Write down how you could fit that into your day.

Heal your emotional wounds
because it helps you live and love better.

Healing from a physical wound allows you to function better physically. The same is true for emotional wounds. The problem with emotional wounds is they are hidden beneath our physical exterior. Many people have emotional wounds from childhood that have yet to be healed. Instead of living their best lives, they suffer from the pain and, in some cases, end up hurting other people. This is why it is important that you invest time, energy, and money to address any emotional wounds you have, no matter how painful. When you complete this process, you can experience life to the fullest. Not only will you experience more peace, happiness, and joy within, but you will find that your relationships with others will improve. Just as you would address a cut on your hand or foot with proper treatment, you should do the same with any deep-rooted emotional wounds you have that are keeping you from living your best life.

My personal application:
After my divorce, I had some emotional wounds that had the potential to ruin my life and my relationship with my children and others. I had bitterness and resentment that I could not shake. As a matter of a fact, I did not want to shake them because it felt good to be in that negative space. Unfortunately, I didn't realize just how much of a negative effect it was having on me. At some point, I had an epiphany and realized I was digging a hole for myself and I had no one to blame but myself. After this realization, I took responsibility for my role in my past pain and future happiness. Although the memories may still linger, the hurt and pain do not affect me in the same way. Moving from the victim role to the victor role helped me heal the emotional wounds and start living the life I was meant to live.

Your challenge / homework:
Identify an emotional wound from which you have not fully healed and that robs you of joy, peace, and happiness. Consider these questions: Do you accept responsibility for your role in the hurt and pain? Do you fully embrace your responsibility in your future happiness and peace of mind? If you answer no to either one of these questions, perhaps this is a starting place for healing your emotional wounds.

<u>Heal</u>

Identify an emotional wound from which you have not fully healed and that robs you of joy, peace, and happiness. Using the space below, consider these questions: Do you accept responsibility for your role in the hurt and pain? Do you fully embrace your responsibility in your future happiness and peace of mind?

<u>Invest</u> in your goals and dreams so they can become a reality.

A successful farmer will tell you that in order to have a great harvest, an investment must be made in advance. This includes time, energy, money, sweat and tears. The same is true for any goal or dream you have in life. There has to be an upfront investment in order for your dream to be realized. Without such an investment, a dream remains just that—a dream. Unfortunately, a lot of dreams don't see the light of day because people don't make the necessary investment. Cars, airplanes, television, eyeglasses, cell phones, and microwaves were all dreams that became a reality because someone made an investment. There are many more advances to be made so we can continue to enjoy life. However, if people are unwilling to make the investment, those advances will never happen. The dream to find a cure to breast cancer can be found if someone is willing to make the investment to do so. Make the investment in your dreams and goals. It will not only change your life, but it could change the world around you.

My personal application:
I started pursuing a doctorate in counseling psychology in 1993 and was dismissed in 2000 for not making satisfactory progress toward completion. The program informed me that I would need to reapply if I wanted to continue working on my doctorate. For 16 years, I wanted to finish the degree. I started and stopped a few times due to my lack of investment. I did not give the goal the time and energy it required. And as expected, the goal was not realized. It was not until I decided to make an investment of time, money, and energy that my goal become a reality. In 2016, I made the necessary investment and in 2020, after more than 20 years, I earned my doctorate. The investment I made was a key factor in reaching my goal.

Your challenge / homework:
What goals and dreams do you have? How will reaching them change your life and the lives of those around you? Are you willing to make the investment? If not, why?

Invest

Using the space below, consider the following questions: what goals and dreams do you have? How will reaching them change your life and the lives of those around you? Are you willing to make the investment? If not, why?

<u>Join</u> a support group because this will improve your mental health and make you feel better.

The benefits of joining a support group, club, or organization are numerous. Some of the benefits include feeling less lonely, isolated or judged; gaining a sense of empowerment and control; improving your coping skills and sense of adjustment; and reducing distress, depression, anxiety or fatigue. For people who are not quite comfortable with seeking individual counseling, a support group can be less intimidating and very effective. A support group is also a great place to gain the proper perspective so you do not feel like you are the only one going through something. Hearing that someone is struggling with a similar issue can be enough to change your perspective from one of feeling alone and isolated to one of feeling connected and supported. Such a shift in thinking can be lifesaving and improve one's overall quality of life and mental health.

My personal application:
Several years ago, I was interested in a support group for individuals who could identify with certain challenges I was having in life and that could serve as a source of support. Initially, I searched around to see if I could find an existing group and was unsuccessful. Thinking outside the box, I decided to start my own support group using the *Meetup* group application. The group was a success. It provided me with the support I needed and allowed me to support others, which was an unexpected benefit.

Your challenge / homework:
Search for a group (via the Internet, the Yellow Pages, or some other resource) that provides the support and affiliation you need and take the steps required to join it. Additionally, if you can't find a group that fits your needs, create or start your own.

Join

Using the space below, research and write down what information you've located about groups you can join that will help support you, and what you need to do to join. If there are no groups that fit your needs, write down what you would do to create your own.

<u>Kiss</u> your past goodbye because a brighter future awaits you.

Everyone has a past they probably would like to forget or erase. The reality is that you cannot simply forget or erase it. However, you do not have to be burdened by it or allow it to keep you from living your best life. Some people have no problem bouncing back after making a big mistake. In fact, some people emerge stronger and better. This is what should happen when something bad happens in your life. You learn from it, and you move forward in the direction of your goals and dreams. One way to kiss your past goodbye is to appreciate that everyone makes mistakes even if they don't admit it. Another approach is to view your mistakes as part of life's classroom and necessary for growth and development. So, starting today, kiss your past goodbye and set your sights on your bright future. The bright future is in front of you, not behind you.

My personal application:
Two major events occurred in my life that had the potential to leave me burdened and bitter. Initially, I blamed other people and was embarrassed by what happened. After a period of digging myself into a pit of pity and bitterness, I came to my senses about what was necessary to move forward and live. Through consistent self-reflection, I accepted responsibility for the things that had occurred in my life. I also made peace with my mistakes and accepted that they will happen no matter how much I try to avoid them. As a result of this step in my healing process, I was able to release the pain of the past and start living without the weight of it. By putting my past in the proper perspective, I have been able to live my life more freely and with less guilt. There are little traces of my past that pop up every now and then, however, they do not take center stage. They are in the background and no longer hold me hostage.

Your challenge/homework:
Identify something from your past that still has a negative impact on your life today, and write it on a blank piece of paper. Under the description of the situation, write the following: "This does not define who I am." "I am bigger and better than the situation or mistake." "I am forgiven and released from the guilt." "I will rise up from this situation/mistake and soar like an eagle." Put this paper in an envelope and store it in a safe place. If you are concerned about someone finding it, shred it and then place it in the envelope. The sheer act of writing your issue on paper will be therapeutic and a step toward putting your past behind you.

<u>Kiss</u>

Identify something from your past that still has a negative impact on your life today, and write it below. Under the description of the situation, write the following: "This does not define who I am." "I am bigger and better than the situation or mistake." "I am forgiven and released from the guilt." "I will rise up from this situation/mistake and soar like an eagle."

Love yourself because it is the first step toward fully loving someone else.

There are a lot of people who do not like themselves. They have issues with their personality, how they look and sound, their height and weight, and the list goes on. This destructive self-loathing comes from negative experiences they have had as well as messages they have received from others in their lives. The consequences of not loving yourself can be dire and affect every aspect of your life, making it virtually impossible to live your best life. Therefore, it is critical that you love yourself and if you don't, you take steps toward that end. Self-love is powerful and will cause you to make decisions that are in your best interest. These types of decisions will improve the quality of your life. The other great thing about loving yourself is that it improves relationships, making you more attractive and easier to love. There is simply no downside to "self-love." With self-love, your potential for living the best life is limitless.

My personal application:
There are a few things about myself that I have not always accepted or embraced. For as long as I can remember, I have always hated the size of my two front teeth, my weight, and my height. Although I was able to experience academic and career success in life, I still didn't really like certain things about myself. The impact was that I was less confident in certain social situations, which affected my relationships. Over time, I have started loving myself more and embracing all my unique features. Although I am not completely where I want to be, I am in a much better place, and I make decisions that are aligned with someone who really loves him or herself.

Your challenge / homework:
Make a list of the things that you do not like about yourself. Indicate why and what messages you have internalized about each one. Speak to a life coach or a counselor about how you can start embracing these aspects of yourself so you can live a more fulfilling life.

<u>Love</u>

Make a list of the things that you do not like about yourself.
Indicate why and what messages you have internalized about each one.

____

____

____

____

____

____

____

____

____

____

____

____

____

____

____

____

____

<u>**Manage**</u> your time, money, emotions, and relationships well because failure to do so can ruin an otherwise good life.

The inability to manage your time, money, emotions, and relationships can have a negative impact on the overall quality of your life. It can ruin your mental and physical health; finances and ability to provide for yourself; personal and professional relationships; career, etc. Unfortunately, these areas are not discussed or taught in school (grade school or college). This omission has dire consequences for everyone because these areas are critical for leading a healthy and balanced life. Therefore, it is critical that you invest time and money in gaining skills in these areas. There are countless classes, books, seminars, workshops and professionals available to assist you in developing skills. The investment you make to develop these skills will have a profound positive effect on your personal and professional life.

My personal application:
Over the years, I have had challenges managing my emotions. For example, when I became upset or anxious, I engaged in emotional eating. There were times I would eat several donuts or pieces of chicken within one sitting. It wasn't because I was hungry; I was dealing with my emotions in a very unhealthy way. I always felt horrible afterwards, and the resulting weight gain compounded the existing problem. It was a vicious cycle. Thankfully, through self-reflection and more self-awareness, I no longer engage in emotional eating. It is so freeing to know that food and emotions do not control me. I am in control, and I do not have to let my emotions dictate what I do.

Your challenge/homework:
Give yourself a grade (A-F) on how well you manage your time, money, emotions, and relationships. Explain why you gave yourself the grades you did and brainstorm one thing you can do to improve your grade in at least one area.

<u>Manage</u>

*List the following categories: Time, Money, Emotions, Relationships.
Give yourself a grade from A – F on how well you believe you manage them. Next
to the grade, explain why you gave yourself the grades you did and brainstorm one
thing you can do to improve your grade
in at least one area.*

<u>Nourish</u> your gift and talent because it produces greatness.

Everyone has a gift or a talent to share with the world to make it a better place. It could be singing, cooking, teaching, playing sports, designing, counseling, speaking, crunching numbers, etc. However, in order for these gifts and talents to be fully realized and utilized, they must be nourished and cultivated. Consider a group of talented athletes who never train or practice. The talent these athletes have will likely benefit them no matter the sport. However, if these same athletes want to maximize their true potential, they will need to devote time to practicing and training for peak performance. Therefore, it is essential that you spend time cultivating and nourishing your gifts and talents through education, training, and practice.

My personal application:
Although I can motivate and encourage people in my sleep, it doesn't mean I am doing my best. In addition to earning several degrees in psychology and counseling and having years of experience, I still avail myself of additional training and experiences. I have joined two life coaching organizations that offer training and support to individuals like me who want to have the edge in their chosen field. Some of the material is a refresher while other content is new. The outcome is that I am positioning myself to be the best and to reach my full potential.

Your challenge/homework:
What are your gifts and talents and how do you nourish them to ensure you are doing your best? If you are not doing anything, what is the reason, and what is one thing you can do to start nourishing your gift or talent?

Nourish

Below, journal what you believe are your gifts and talents and how do you nourish them, or plan to nourish them, to ensure you are doing your best?

<u>**Open**</u> your mouth and speak up because your life
and future depend on it.

I t's true, there's a time to speak and there is a time to be quiet or silent. The times when you need to speak up are typically when you don't necessarily feel like it or you feel intimidated or even embarrassed. An old saying is, "A closed mouth is never fed." When you are in situations where there is a chance for a positive outcome, but you are afraid to speak, this is when you need to say something. It could be raising your hand in class to get clarification about a concept you don't understand; sharing a concern with someone who cares and can help; asking for a raise at work; or even asking someone out for a date. Yes, the outcome could be negative. However, if you don't speak up, it will definitely be so. Therefore, muster up the courage in these types of situations and speak up. There is a good chance you will get the outcome you want. Even if you don't, you will have the experience that will build your confidence for similar situations in the future.

My personal application:

Recently, I was contemplating launching a business selling slices of cake. I wanted to launch the business at a local site that already gets a lot of traffic. I knew of the perfect place, I just needed to approach the owners to see if they would allow me to sell my cake outside their business. Initially, I was afraid to ask because I didn't want to hear "no." This delayed my asking them for several weeks. At some point and after some self-coaching, I finally reached out to the owners via a social media messenger and stated my request. I never received a written response to my message. However, about three weeks later, one of the owners paid me a visit. The owner indicated that his wife had received my request and that I could sell my cakes outside their business, free of charge. To think, if I had given into my fears I would have missed a golden opportunity to take my cake business to the next level.

Your challenge / homework:

What is one thing you should speak up about but have not done so because of fear? Where does the fear come from? Set a goal of speaking up the next time you are given the opportunity to do so and note the results. As the saying goes, no risk, no reward.

<u>Open</u>

What is one thing you should speak up about but have not done so because of fear? Where does the fear come from? Write down a goal of speaking up the next time you are given the opportunity to do so and note the results.

Practice patience daily because nothing great happens in an instant.

I cannot overstate the importance of being patient in life. One problem with not being patient is missing opportunities that await you. The other problem is the negative impact it has on your relationships. When you are impatient, you become overly demanding and have unrealistic expectations of others. This can ruin relationships. The way that society is set up does not help with patience either, everything is about speed and instant gratification. We have in essence become a microwave-society. Although there are benefits to getting things done quickly, some things cannot and should not be rushed. The birthing process, for example, takes nine months. You cannot rush this. Obtaining a degree and losing weight are other examples. Therefore, it is imperative that we practice patience daily in order to experience meaningful and significant things in life. One example of practicing patience is delaying your responses. Instead of responding to someone immediately, give it a few minutes or even a few days. Another technique is to keep your eye on the big picture in every situation. This allows you to overlook some of the nuisances that come with reaching a goal or completing a task. Finally, practicing patience requires faith. You must trust the process and appreciate that the universe is working to help you win.

My personal application:
Last year, after recognizing that my being impatient was preventing me from reaching significant goals and having a better quality of life, I made a decision to practice more patience. My current weight loss journey has required patience. There were times when I did not see the results I thought I should. Instead of giving up, I used my journal to document what was going on in my life, vent about my frustration, and note my successes. As a result, I have stayed the course despite fluctuations on the scale and have been able to keep the weight off longer than I have ever in my entire life. Practicing patience works!

Your challenge/homework:
Identify an area in which you need to practice more patience and incorporate a strategy that requires you to delay your response. Practice this strategy for at least 20 days and note any changes that occurred as a result of your practicing more patience.

<u>Practice</u>

Identify an area in which you need to practice more patience and write down your strategy that requires you to delay your response. After 20 days, note any changes that occurred as a result.

Quit quitting because you will never win!

Starting a project or a task is really easy, right? Yes. The hard part is finishing it. Some early research by psychologists indicated that nearly a quarter of adults around the world have issues completing what they start. Why might this be the case? There are several reasons. Some of these include 1) underestimating the amount of time a project takes, 2) wanting a project to be perfect, 3) fear of being evaluated, and 4) lack of confidence. Determining the reason why you have difficulty finishing tasks is the first step toward getting more done. With this knowledge, you can develop a plan to address the underlying cause of your not finishing what you start. The saying is very true: winners never quit.

My personal application:
Quitting or not finishing what I start is something I have done more than I would like to admit. You name it, from starting businesses and not following through to reading only the first few pages of a new book. On the surface, this may seem harmless. However, this pattern I adopted was costly on many levels. For businesses, I missed opportunities to make additional income to support my family. When I failed to finish a book I selected, I missed opportunities for personal and professional development. To combat this counterproductive pattern, I started using strategies to help me finish what I start. For example, I overestimate the time required for a task and I also give myself permission to complete tasks that are less than perfect. These strategies have helped me finish more and increased my productivity level.

Your challenge / homework:
If you have a list of things that you have not completed, take a moment to explore the reasons. Consider the reasons discussed here, and consider taking steps to address the cause so you can achieve more in life.

Quit

Write out a list of tasks or goals that you have not completed and take a moment to explore the reasons. Explore and write out what steps you could take to address the cause(s) so you can achieve more in life.

Read or recite something motivational each morning before you start your day because it programs your brain for success.

We learned very early that reading is fundamental and a building block for learning. Well, reading something inspirational or motivational is fundamental to success in life. I equate this exercise to filling your car up with gas before taking a trip. This type of exercise is important because things happen during the course of a day that can easily throw you off track. Some people can bounce back and keep moving after an upsetting event. Other people are thrown off track and find it almost impossible to keep moving. What's the difference here? Some people maintain a winning mindset that is fueled by their positive thoughts, while the others are derailed by their negative, self-defeating thoughts. When we are thrown off track by life and find it difficult to continue moving in the direction of our dreams and goals, the consequences are dire. We forfeit important goals and dreams that are designed to change not only our lives but also the lives of our families and communities. This is why it is important to develop mental muscle and fortitude by feeding your mind and spirit each day with positive information. Winning in life is not about having a problem-free life. Nope. It's about responding to life's situations in ways that move you forward. Winning requires that you have the right mindset. This mindset can be established by the information we take in each and every day.

My personal application:
Although I am generally positive, my mind still needs nourishment. I have situations from time to time that are very challenging. I might even question my worth or value and want to give up. By reading motivational information and reciting a positive mantra at the start of each day, I put myself in a position to handle the challenges that arise. It's similar to eating breakfast, which can help you get through the day. Additionally, there are times when I refer to my motivational messages (written on index cards) throughout the day for reinforcement, especially after an unexpected and challenging situation pops up. My positive messages help me stay centered and focused on my goals and dreams. To be honest, I am not sure where I would be without my positive messages. When I am especially bothered by a situation, a quick read through my messages usually helps me get my mental footing so I can push through and win.

Your challenge/homework:
If your daily routine doesn't include reading or reciting something motivational or inspirational before you start each day, what is one thing you can read or recite starting today? Do this for 21 days and note the impact this exercise has on your life.

<u>Read or recite</u>

List or research inspirational material that you can read before you start your day, or recite at the beginning of your day. Once you've located your material, start your day with either reading or reciting it. Do this for 21 days and note the impact this exercise has on your life.

<u>Stay</u> in your lane because it's less crowded.

Staying in your lane doesn't mean limiting yourself or making yourself invisible. It means that you intentionally engage in activities and projects that are aligned with your gifts, talents, values, and interests. Some of us, for various reasons, become involved in things that are not a good fit for us. When this happens, the outcome can cause unnecessary frustration and result in missed opportunities to reach our full potential in life. Perhaps family members suggested that you pursue a particular degree in college because of their personal experience. A close friend could have suggested that you become his or her business partner based solely on your friendship. Although these are nice gestures, they may not be right for you. Finding your lane and staying in it will take a little homework and courage. However, it will pay off in the long run. You will undoubtedly experience more personal and professional success. You will also feel a great sense of fulfillment because you are doing the thing that feels most natural.

My personal application:
I will be the first to admit that I have not always travelled in my lane. I have been in the wrong lane several times because something looked or sounded good or someone suggested it. For example, back in 1998 I took a job as a 5th grade teacher. My original plan was to teach for a few years and then move into administration. However, deep down inside, I wanted to be working with people as a counselor and a life coach. Because I pursued something that was not completely aligned with my goals and interests, I was very unhappy and did not feel fulfilled. Consequently, I resigned before the school year ended. Today, my full-time job involves counseling, advising, teaching, and motivating others, and I absolutely love it. As a matter of fact, I get energy from what I do and I never, ever get tired. This is all because I am operating and travelling in my lane.

Your challenge/homework:
Are you operating and functioning in your lane personally and professionally? If so, how do you know this? If you are not, explain why and what steps you can take to engage in activities that are more aligned with your interests and values.

<u>Stay</u>

Below, write down if you believe you are operating and functioning in your lane personally and professionally. If so, how do you know this? If you are not, explain why and what steps you can take to engage in activities that are more aligned with your interests and values.

<u>Trust</u> yourself because it is the cornerstone for your self-esteem and confidence.

Second-guessing yourself happens when you don't trust or have confidence in yourself. It is a form of insecurity that some people experience when thinking about whether they will make the right decision or have made the right decision. Second-guessing typically starts at a young age when you are made to feel like you are not enough or that you are not capable of making good, sound decisions. Although this mental paralysis typically starts at an early age and can have lingering effects, it doesn't have to ruin your life. You can take steps to build your self-confidence so second-guessing becomes a thing of the past. It may require you to explore with a counselor the reasons you don't trust yourself. This process will likely bring up some hurtful memories from the past. However, once these things are discussed and dealt with properly, you will be well on your way to trusting yourself more and enjoying your life as intended. Your life will be fueled by your self-confidence and no longer plagued by second-guessing.

My personal application:
Unfortunately, I have been impacted by second-guessing throughout my life. It can be very stressful and have a negative impact on every aspect of your life. This includes personal and professional relationships, finances, and your mental and physical health. Thankfully, I discovered success builds confidence, which helps with second-guessing. I started working on a doctorate back in 1993 and did not complete it. It haunted me and I felt like a failure because of it. This resulted in my not feeling really good about myself and a lot of second-guessing. The result was a life that was not lived to the fullest. So after 25 years, I decided to finish what I started. When I completed my doctorate, it boosted my self-confidence in an unexpected way. Although I am not completely out of the woods, second guessing no longer impacts me in the way that it did. My improved self-confidence has improved my relationships and productivity.

Your challenge/homework:
Do you second-guess yourself often? If so, where do you think it comes from? Consider exploring this with a counselor so the quality of your life can be improved.

<u>Trust</u>

Using the space below, explore whether you believe you second-guess yourself often, and where you believe it comes from. Can you pin-point the first time you started second-guessing yourself? What led to that, and how you use this insight to combat that?

<u>Understand</u> others and their uniqueness because
it reduces stress and improves relations.

Although it is obvious that no two people are alike, we sometimes interact with others as though this is the case. Physiologically, we are essentially the same. However, beyond this, we are very different. The differences among us come from the varying experiences we have in life. How we think, feel, and interact with others are influenced and shaped by these experiences. In an ideal world, everyone understands and appreciates each other's differences and there is harmony. In less than ideal situations, differences are not celebrated and embraced and conflicts arise. Some of the conflicts can be attributed to people not understanding and appreciating others. Since interacting with others is an important function of daily living, and it is important for our overall well-being, it is critical that we take deliberate steps to understand others. We do not have to agree with their feelings or point of view. Instead, we should recognize their point of view, and accept that it is different from ours. We can experience more peace personally and will undoubtedly create more harmony in the world.

My personal application:
Several years ago, I recognized that each of my children has a unique personality. With this recognition, I also started to embrace and celebrate their uniqueness. I stopped treating them like robots and computers that required programming. Unfortunately, I was convinced that I needed to create mini versions of myself in order for them to be successful in life. Needless to say, I was frustrated when my efforts to mold them didn't work. Thankfully, despite how I might feel about some of the things they do, I allow them to be themselves. I guide them when appropriate and find ways to accentuate the positive and redirect any problematic behavior. My understanding and appreciating my children's uniqueness has improved our relationships tremendously.

Your challenge / homework:
Identify someone or a group of people that you do not like or understand. Explore how you might get to know this person or group better. This month, take one step toward getting to know this person or group and report the impact of this understanding on the relationship.

<u>Understand</u>

Using the space below, identify someone or a group of people that you do not like or understand. Write out how you might get to know that person or group better.

<u>Vent</u> because it helps you see things more clearly.

When speaking of a mechanical system, venting allows "fresh" outdoor air to come in and "contaminated" air to be removed. This is an important health and safety function. Similarly, venting about issues and concerns in our lives does the same thing. The type of venting of which I am speaking involves writing about your emotions, feelings or thoughts in a journal. Writing things down is a healthy way to express yourself and can help you manage anxiety, reduce stress, and cope with depression. Venting in a journal can also help you improve your mood by giving you the opportunity to prioritize your problems, fears, and concerns in a way that makes them more manageable. Moreover, you can identify a problem, its source, and work on a strategy or a plan of action to address it. Finally, holding things in has been related to compromised health— physical, mental, and emotional. This outcome further supports the need to vent.

My personal application:
While I was going through my divorce, I started journaling as a way to reflect on some very painful and perplexing situations. At the time, there were things going on that I did not feel comfortable or safe discussing with anyone else. The journal allowed me to pour out my soul without fear of judgment or rejection. I was able to release and then reflect with a clearer head because I had reduced my issues and concerns to writing. I have now been journaling for over 10 years and have over 30 composition books as proof. Today, I find myself venting in my journal two or three times a day, depending on what's going on. My mood and state of mind always improve after I journal. I write about family, health, career, financial, mental health, and relationship issues as well as my dreams. At the end of each venting session, I typically list action items. As such, my journal acts as a life coach of sorts without the added cost. I can say without a doubt that venting in my journal has been a game changer and a lifesaver.

Your challenge / homework:
Purchase four or five composition books and commit to venting in them for a month. You can start by reflecting on the two or three areas of your life. You can write about what went well, not so well, and what could have been done differently. Make note in your journal about the journaling experience and its effects. If you found it helpful, continue journaling to improve your overall health.

<u>Vent</u>

Start the venting process by reflecting on the two or three areas of your life below. You can write about what went well, not so well, and what could have been done differently. If this is helpful, consider starting to journal daily to improve your overall health.

Write down your goals and dreams because it serves as a road map.

If you want to increase your chances of reaching your goals in life, you simply need to write them down. It is perfectly fine to daydream and visualize about the future you want. However, putting what's in your head on paper is one of the keys to goals becoming a reality. A Harvard Business Study found that 3% of their MBA graduates who had their goals written down ended up earning ten times as much as the other 97% put together, just ten years after graduation. Since everyone wants to make their dreams a reality, the practice of writing down important goals should be the rule and not the exception. Written goals serve as a blueprint for you to follow and give you a way to track your progress, which is essential to reaching any goal. As the saying goes, if the goal isn't written down, it isn't real, and therefore not achievable.

My personal application:
I had three major goals over the last several years and each one of them has been accomplished. These included earning my doctorate, losing 20 pounds, and moving into my own place. Each one of these goals was written down in my yearly planner and posted on the back of my bedroom door. Although there were many hiccups along the way, having them written down helped me stay on track and focus. I am positive I would not have reached these goals had they not been written. The written goals served as physical reminders and road maps for my goals.

Your challenge / homework:
What things would you like to accomplish before you die, in 10 years, 5 years, 1-3 years, and within the next three months? Write your goals in your journal and use the journal as your planning tool to guide you toward reaching all your goals in life.

Write

Write your goals out for the next three months, 1-3 years, 5 years, and 10 years below. Let writing them out serve as the starting point to help you reaching your goals.

<u>**X-ray**</u> what's going wrong in your life and deal with it because living a free life depends on it.

An actual x-ray is a type of radiation that has electromagnetic waves that create pictures of the inside of your body to provide insight about certain health issues. Metaphorically speaking, it is important, especially when things are not going right, for us to take a deeper look to determine what might be the underlying issue. Therefore, it is important to stop and take a look at things an x-ray does. The x-ray looks beneath the surface to uncover things that might be causing problems outwardly. When we fail to do such an investigation, our issues can become our Achilles Heel, a small but fatal weakness, so to speak. X-raying your issues can be done through personal reflection or by speaking with a professional counselor.

My personal application:
Over the years, I have learned that some of my insecurities are related to certain childhood experiences. In particular, I can be extremely sensitive to criticism from others. Before my awareness of the source of my insecurities, I would overreact by being defensive or becoming extremely upset and discouraged. Although these insecurities are not completely erased, my awareness has helped me regulate/temper my responses. My relationships and productivity have improved when working with others, both socially and professionally. Doing an x-ray of my underlying issues significantly improved the quality of my life.

Your challenge/homework:
What are some negative emotions or reactions you have to situations in your life? Are you clear on why you have the reactions you do? Do some reflecting or speak to a professional counselor to get a better understanding of the origin of your negative emotions and reactions. The discovery will put you one step closer to living your best life.

X-ray

Using the space below, write out your most frequent negative emotions or your most recent reaction to a negative situation in your life. Are you clear on why you have reacted in this way? Explore below what might have caused your reaction.

<u>Yield</u> (surrender) to win because being in control is not always required.

For some of us, yielding or surrendering to win sounds counterintuitive. I completely understand. However, there is something powerful about yielding and letting go in certain situations. It takes a certain level of confidence and faith to experience the best life—one that is filled with more peace and abundance. Yielding is important because many times it is the one thing keeping a roadblock in place. Most of us want to control everything in our lives; however, for some situations to improve, we must step back completely. We must let go of the tight grip and surrender. At this moment, other forces can operate freely. As a result, we can experience unexpected peace and freedom that can be transformative and life-changing. Although the situation may not turn out completely as we expect, the yielding will put us in a better position to handle the situation and the outcome.

My personal application:
Yielding is an ongoing process for me. However, in one area yielding has been particularly helpful. Over the last several years, I have had some professional challenges to maneuver. It was my learning to yield and let go of the need to control that helped me win big in a particularly challenging situation. The situation involved a new job in which I was interested. I did everything according to the book, and it did not work according to my plan. Instead of reacting as I normally would with telephone calls, emails, and other control tactics, I consciously stepped back. I did not do anything in response to the outcome in the situation. As it turned out, my yielding was the perfect prescription for other opportunities that presented themselves. I am so grateful that I have learned to yield. It's a silent act of faith that continues to prove beneficial in every area of my life.

Your challenge/homework:
Identify something you are holding onto with a tight grip and trying to control because of fear and a lack of faith. What is one thing you can do to start yielding and letting go so you can experience more peace and success?

<u>Yield</u>

Identify below at least one thing that you are holding onto tightly, or trying to control due to lack of fear and faith. What is one way you can start letting go of this fear to help improve your sense of peace and mental health?

<u>Zip</u> your lips because everything doesn't require a response.

"Zip your lips" is something you might hear a parent or teacher tell a child who is talking too much. Although it seems appropriate for an adult to tell a child, sometimes these words apply to adults. Sometimes we talk too much. When we do, we miss important information and sabotage opportunities. Silence is golden, especially when you are trying to build relationships and achieve important things in life. When I was growing up, I used to hear my preacher say, "To everything there is a season and a time to every purpose under the heavens." As such, there is a time to speak and there is a time to be silent. When we learn the art of being silent or zipping our lips, the quality of our lives will improve and new opportunities will emerge.

My personal application:
"Wise men speak because they have something to say; fools because they have to say something." ~ Plato. I must admit that I have been a fool in my day. I have spoken when I really didn't have anything to say. I had nervous energy and felt the need to fill the empty space with words. I also thought it somehow added value to who I was. I was dead, dead, and dead wrong. I actually talked myself out of several opportunities and into hot water in others. Today, I listen more and speak less. People who know me have commented on the difference in my behavior. I am confident this difference has improved my personal and professional relationships.

Your challenge/homework:
If you are a very talkative person and find yourself talking in social situations because of anxiety, practice allowing at least 10 to 20 seconds between you and the other person talking. Make a note of how it felt and any benefits you found.

<u>Zip</u>

Using the space below, journal how it felt to sit in the silence between yourself and the other person. Were there benefits you found to letting yourself engage in thoughtful conversation and not letting your anxiety get the better of you?

About the Author

Thomas Chatman, Jr. (50) is a native of Moyock, NC and a graduate of Elizabeth City State University (BS, Elementary Education and Psychology), the University of Minnesota (MA, Counseling Psychology), Virginia Commonwealth University (Certificate, Public Management), and Liberty University (Doctorate, Counseling and Family and Marriage Therapy). His work experience includes working as an elementary school teacher, guidance officer, department manager, motivational speaker, professor, minister, and counselor.

Dr. Chatman is currently the Dean of Student Support Services/Campus Dean at Tidewater Community College and has been employed at the college for 15 years. During his tenure, he has held various positions to include psychology instructor, program coordinator, and counselor. He has a passion for helping students and staff reach their full potential. He has been recognized for making significant contributions to the college's mission as well as for his innovative approaches to addressing student success and retention issues.

Dr. Chatman is a devoted father to three children (21, 20, and 17) and enjoys spending time with his family, cooking, writing, working on small home projects, fishing, and inspiring others to live their best life. Dr. Chatman also owns a baking business where he specializes in pound cakes.